The
Book
of
Riddles

This edition published in 2016 by
CHARTWELL BOOKS
an imprint of Book Sales
a division of Quarto Publishing Group USA Inc.
142 West 36th Street, 4th Floor
New York, New York 10018
USA

English translation by Tom Clegg

Letter 'R' illustration on front cover
and title page © 1999 Pepin van Roojen

ISBN 978-0-7858-3455-7

Printed in China

The Book of Riddles

Fabrice Mazza
Sylvain Lhullier
Illustrations by Ivan Sigg

CHARTWELL
BOOKS

CONTENTS

NTRODUCTION - TO THE READER

Is there anyone out there who doesn't enjoy challenging their friends' minds with a brain-teasing enigma - especially one that may leave them completely flummoxed?

The tradition of enigmas dates back millennia. They have been passed on, transformed and enriched over the years in countless homes, as well as through myths, literature and in our own times, the Internet.

I have selected the best and most amusing enigmas of a certain type, ones that require inventiveness, shrewdness and wisdom to solve.

Because the pleasure of a good enigma lies in seeking... but also in finding - and finding on your own - the path to the solution. No two people arrive at the solution in the same way, and therein lies the interest in sharing these puzzles with friends. So I urge you, dear reader, not to look at the answers except in case of imminent cerebral meltdown.

This book is intended to carry on the tradition of enigmas: now it is up to you to pass them on, transform them and further enrich them.

Happy reading, and happy hunting!

Fabrice Mazza

RIDDLES

 INSHIP BOND

You ask yourself this:
"I am a man. If the son of this other man is the father of my son, what is the bond of kinship between this man and myself?"

Solution on page 90

MILLION HAIRS

Before the Black Death ravaged Europe in the 14th century, the kingdom of France had about sixteen million inhabitants, and none of them possessed more than a million hairs on their head.

Can one be certain that there were at least two inhabitants in the kingdom who had exactly the same number of hairs on their head?

Solution on page 91

ANUSCRIPT

A cleric must number the pages of a manuscript from 1 to 100.
How many times will he inscribe the figure 9?

Solution on page 92

ABRIC CLIPPING

When do the diagonal lines on this swatch of fabric meet?

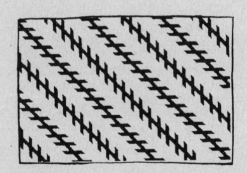

Solution on page 93

SOLATION

At the hospital, a patient has come down with the plague.

To prevent it from spreading, it's been decided that the patients in the common ward should be separated with the help of two screens, each in the form of a square, which can be of any size.

How should these two square screens be placed in order to isolate each patient?

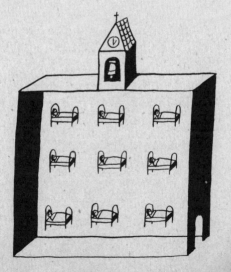

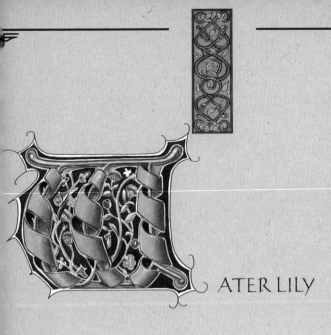

ATER LILY

A water lily doubling its surface area every year covers an entire pond at the end of ten years.

If there had been two water lilies with the same properties, how much time would it have taken to cover the pond entirely?

Solution on page 95

WOUND

During a tournament, a man and his son are both competing. A lance impales the father, who dies on the spot.

His son, also wounded, is carried into a tent.

The doctor charged with examining him leans over the stretcher and exclaims, 'Good heavens! It's my son!'

How can this be?

Solution on page 96

 ATS

If, in the kitchens of the castle, three cats catch three mice in 3 minutes, how many cats are needed to catch one hundred mice in 100 minutes?

3 minutes

Solution on page 97

TOURNAMENT

On your way to a tournament, you meet six knights, each accompanied by six squires. Each squire leads two horses by the reins, and on each horse are seated two young children.

How many people and animals are going to the tournament?

Solution on page 98

ATCH TRIANGLES 1

How can the carpenter's apprentice at the building site in Catfisher Street create eight equilateral trangles with six matches?

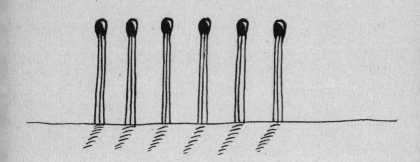

Solution on page 99

ATCH TRIANGLES 2

At the cathedral building site, a journeyman wonders, during his break, how he might form four equilateral triangles with six matches.

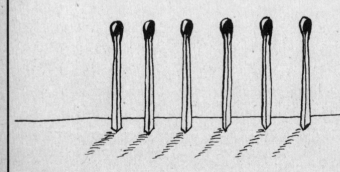

ICIOUS CIRCLE

Write out the missing figure in letters, while preserving the coherence of the sentence.

In this circle the "r" is present ... times

Solution on page 101

HE MONK AND THE MOUNTAIN

As penitence for breaking silence during supper, a monk has to climb a mountain. He leaves in the morning at 9am and arrives at the summit by 12 noon. He rests overnight, sleeping under the stars, and starts back down at 9am the next morning. Following the same path in reverse, he arrives at the bottom by 11am. Is there any point along this route where he finds himself in the same place at the same time on both days?

How can you prove the existence or non-existence of such a point?

TRANGE EQUIVALENCE

In what period of history might this equivalence be said to be true?

$$31_{OCT} = 25_{DEC}$$

Solution on page 103

 OVE POTION

Merlin must prepare a love potion for King Arthur. According to his book of magic spells, he needs 4 fluid ounces of oil of toad.

To measure volumes, the wizard only has two unmarked jars, one of them containing 5 fl oz, the other 3 fl oz.
How can he measure 4 fl oz?

Solution on page 104

UESTION OF AGE

A master asks his pupil:

'I am four times as old as you were when I was the same age as you are now. I am forty years old, how old are you?'

Solution on page 105

HIELD OF NAILS

How can this shield be divided into four exactly equal zones, each containing the same number of nails?

Solution on page 106

 UT-UP SQUARE

How can you turn the cross on this armour into a square with just two scissor cuts, knowing that you can move the pieces about?

 INGLE FILE

King Arthur set a challenge for four of the Knights of the Round Table:

'I'm going to put you in a line, and you musn't turn around or communicate with one another.'

A tapestry is placed between Lancelot and the others. Lancelot and Galahad can't see any of the other three.

Percival can see Galahad, and Gawain can see Percival and Galahad.

'I have here four helmets, two of them with a white feather on top, two with a black feather. Close your eyes while I place them on your heads. If one of you can tell me the colour of the feather on top of his own helmet, that knight will win Excalibur!'

They open their eyes, and after a few moments' reflection, one of the four knights finds the correct answer.

Which knight won Excalibur? And how did he know the colour of the feather on the top of his helmet?

Solution on page 108

 UT-UP

Cut this headdress up into four superimposable parts.

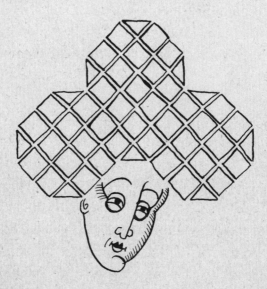

Solution on page 109

ELLS

Quasimodo, the bell ringer of Notre-Dame cathedral in Paris, takes three seconds to ring four o'clock.

How long does it take him to ring midday?

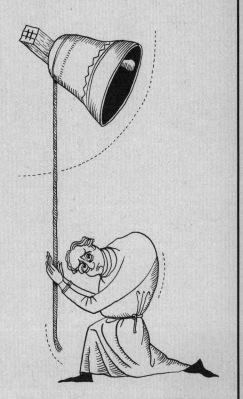

Solution on page 110

 IVE SQUARES

A troubadour at the fair has created a figure formed by five squares.

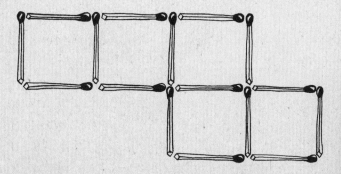

How does he form four squares of the same size by moving just two matches?

 HILDREN

Godfrey de Bouillon has five children. Half of them are daughters.

How can this be?

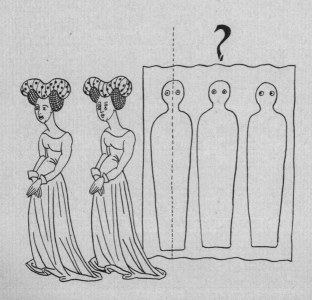

 LOCK

Aucassin has one of the very first models of a verge-and-foliot clock. He never abandons it completely, but often forgets to wind it up.

Whenever it stops, he goes to the porch of the cathedral (whose façade includes a clock) to find Nicolette, the young Saracen women with whom he has fallen in love, then goes back home and resets his clock to the correct time.

How does he manage this, given that he does not know the length of his journey, but knows that he walks as fast on the way to the cathedral as he does on the return journey?

 ALUE OF THE
PRODUCT

What is the value of the following product :
$(x - a) (x - b) (x - c) (x - d) (x - y) (x - z)$?

There are in all 26 parentheses, and a, b ... z can be any numbers (real or complex).

Solution on page 114

IVE ALIGNMENTS

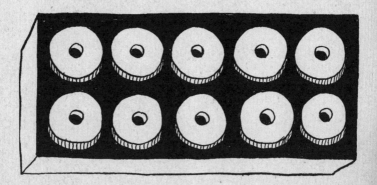

Arrange these ten pieces to form five lines of four pieces each.

Solution on page 115

ROSE WINDOW

Looking at the rose window of the cathedral, Friar Francis wonders, 'Which grey circle is bigger, the one above or the one below?'

EADDRESS

In a room without any light are three black headdresses and two white ones.

Three ladies of the court are allowed entry, the last of whom is blind. Each of them takes a headdress at random and places it on her head. The two remaining headdresses are removed.

Candles are lit and each lady is asked whether she is capable of guessing the colour of her headdress.

The first lady looks at the two others and says, 'NO.'

The second lady also looks at the two others and answers, 'NO.'

The third, despite being blind, answers, 'YES.'

How has this blind lady correctly guessed the colour of her headdress?

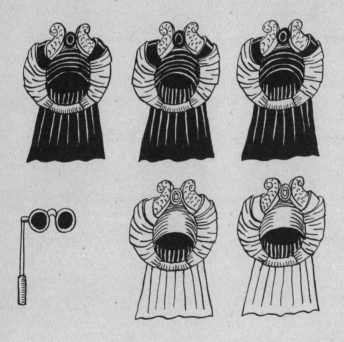

Solution on page 117

HE GUARDS' HALL

In the Guards' Hall, six hundred men wait to be sent off to war. Among them, 5% have one weapon. Among the remaining 95%, half of them bear two weapons, while the others have none. How many weapons are there in total within the Guards' Hall?

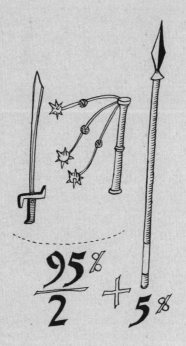

$$\frac{95\%}{2} + 5\%$$

ROUBADOUR

A troubadour holding three objects (a ball, a hat and a bowling pin) arrives at a bridge. The bridgekeeper warns him, 'The bridge won't bear more than your weight plus a maximum of two objects, and it's not possible to throw the objects over to the far side.'

The troubadour nevertheless manages to get to the other side carrying his three objects in a single crossing.

How does he do it?

Solution on page 119

 ISH

This fish composed of eight matches is swimming to the right. By shifting three matches, make it swim to the left.

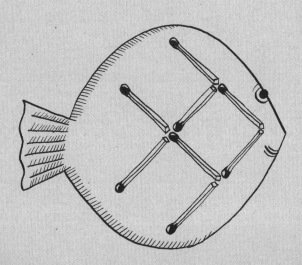

Solution on page 120

RIANGLE TEASER

Fill in this triangle so that the number inscribed in each space is equal to the sum of the two numbers inscribed in the two spaces immediately below it.

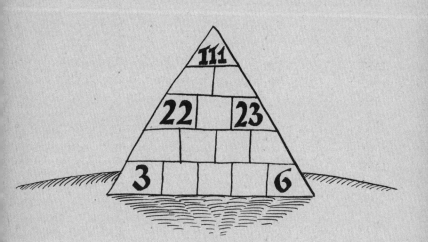

Solution on page 121

CCURRENCES

King Dagobert is absent-minded, and has forgotten the code for the strongbox in which he keeps his royal regalia.

He goes to see Saint Éloi, his treasurer, to whom he remembers having confided something that will jog his memory, just in case. The saint hands him a parchment which reads:

'To recover the code for the strongbox, you need to replace the blanks in the following sentence with numbers; in such a way that the sentence shall remain coherent (the inserted numbers also being counted). The ten inserted numbers, in order, shall provide the code.'

Here is the sentence:

'In this sentence, the number of occurrences of 0 is _, of 1 is _, of 2 is _, of 3 is _, of 4 is _, of 5 is _, of 6 is _, of 7 is _, of 8 is _, and of 9 is _.'

What is the code King Dagobert must apply in order to open the strongbox and retrieve his crown?

Solution on page 122

HREE-WAY GAME

Three fellows, Martin, Eberulf and Leander, are finishing a game that is played in five rounds. They have been betting with 1-shilling pieces and throughout the game have only played with amounts in whole numbers.

In each round, the loser has doubled the holdings of the two other players. At the end of the game, Martin has 8 shillings, Eberulf has 9, and Leander has 10.

How much did each player have at the start of the game?

Solution on page 123

A PLACE OF THEIR OWN

A copyist proposes rearranging seating in the Illuminations Hall.

Lady Clarissa wants to sit behind Friar Stephen, but the latter won't hear of it: it will be he who sits behind Lady Clarissa!

How do they resolve the problem?

Solution on page 124

HREE SWISS

Three Swiss share a brother. When this brother dies, the three Swiss no longer have a brother.

How is this possible, knowing that it is not a question of a half-brother?

Solution on page 125

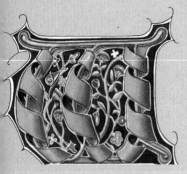 ATER IN THE WINE

You have two perfectly identical mugs; one contains 15 fl oz of wine, the other 15 fl oz of water.

You take a spoonful from the water mug and empty it into the mug of wine before mixing it thoroughly.

Next, you fill the same spoon from this second mug and empty it into the first. So once again, you have 15 fl oz of liquid in each mug.

Which of them has more water in the wine, or wine in the water?

Solution on page 126

WHAT DAY?

If today isn't the day after Monday or the day before Thursday, if tomorrow isn't Sunday, if it wasn't Sunday yesterday, and if the day before yesterday wasn't Wednesday, what day is it today?

ATCHES

How does one obtain four identical squares that touch one another from these five squares, by moving only three matches?

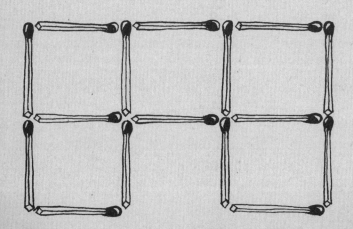

Solution on page 128

 USES

Merlin must let a potion settle for exactly 45 minutes, but he has no device for measuring time.

On the other hand, he does have a torch and two fuses, which he knows burn in 1 hour, but in an irregular fashion (half of a fuse will not be consumed in 30 minutes).

How can the wizard measure exactly 45 minutes?

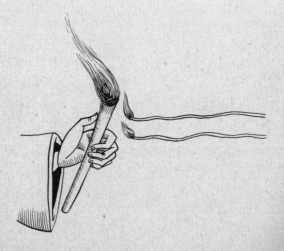

TANDARD

Here is a battle standard composed of eight squares arranged in the following manner:

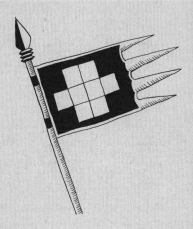

Place each of the numbers running from 1 to 8 in the squares of the standard so than none of the numbers is in contact on any side or diagonally with another number that directly precedes it or follows it.

Hint:
Two of the numbers have a characteristic that is distinct from the other six.

Solution on page 130

PAVED COURTYARD

In this courtyard, how would you describe the lines?

 EAR HUNT

A hunter seeks to kill a bear. He spots one and wants to take it by surprise. In order to go around it, the hunter travels on foot 5 miles to the south, then 5 miles east, and finally 5 miles north... And there, much to his dismay, he finds himself face-to-face with the bear, which has not moved at all.

Question:
What colour is the bear?

Solution on page 132

ARSENIC

The queen wants to get rid of the king's favourite. Taking advantage of the fact that her rival is ill and must take a medicinal pill each day, she calls on the services of a poisoner, to whom she passes twelve boxes of twelve pills, to be replaced by poison.

But the old witch dies before she can complete her sinister task, and she has only had time to substitute arsenic pills for the twelve pills contained in one box.

The queen knows that the arsenic pills weigh 1 oz less than the others, which weigh 10 oz. How can she, with the help of a steelyard (a balance with only one tray), find the box that has been tampered with?

ISHING

Two fathers accompanied by their respective sons go fishing.
Each person catches a fish. Yet only three fish are caught.
Why?

 ONNECTIONS

Here are two houses, M1 and M2.

You need to connect them to electricity (A), gas (B), and water (C), knowing that:

- each of these three services (A, B, and C) must be connected to each of the two houses (M1 and M2);

- the lines must not touch or cross, but they can be long and curvy.

Solution on page 135

ROMAN NUMERAL EQUATION 1

Look at this equation:

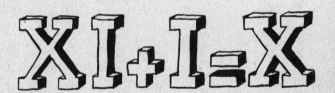

$$XI + I = X$$

What do you need to do, without modifying the terms, to make this equation valid?

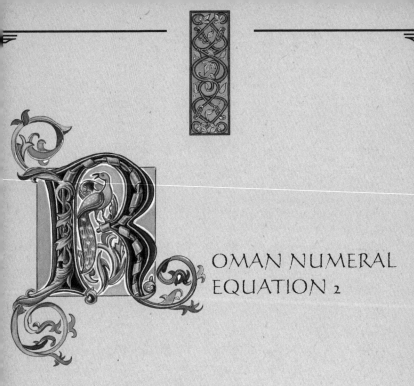

ROMAN NUMERAL EQUATION 2

Here is another strange equation:

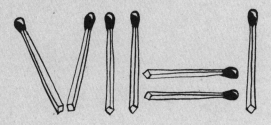

What do you need to do, by moving just one match, to make this equation valid (other than simply crossing the '=' sign to make '≠')?

RIANGLE AND SUMS

Place two numbers from 4 to 9 on each side of this triangle so that the sum of each side is equal to 17.

Be careful! You can only use each number once (and 1, 2, and 3 are already in place).

 OUNT THE TRIANGLES

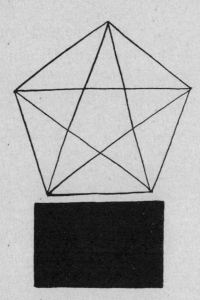

Gazing at a multifaceted jewel resting on its base, the king's steward asks himself, 'How many triangles are there?'

Solution on page 139

LAZIERS

Two master glaziers are competing to make the stained glass windows for Chartres cathedral. To decide which one will be awarded the job, the archbishop issues them with the following challenge:

'Here is a square of glass with sides measuring 12 inches and a ring with a diameter of 2½ inches. He who manages to cut the glass into four equal pieces so that they can slip through the ring without breaking will be given the task.'

How should they proceed given that each has a diamond allowing them to cut the glass in any direction?

Solution on page 140

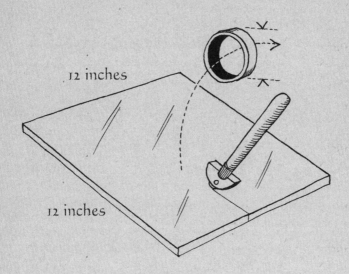

12 inches

12 inches

ASSWORD

A papal legate wants to attend a secret meeting being held by heretical Cathar knights. To be admitted, he must give a password to the guard at the door. He hides nearby and listens as other people show up.

A man arrives. The guard says to him, 'Five,' the man replies, 'Four,' and the guard allows him to pass. A second man turns up. The guard says to him, 'Six,' to which he replies, 'Three,' and is allowed through. A last man appears. The guard says to him, 'Four,' he responds, 'Four,' and enters. Now it's the papal legate's turn. The guard says to him, 'Seven.' What should he answer to gain entry?

Solution on page 141

OME MENTAL CALCULATIONS

We can use four 1s in an equation to produce quite different totals:

1 1 1 1 = 3

1 1 1 1 = 4

using different arithmetical operations to arrive at the correct result:

$1 + 1 + (1 \times 1) = 3$

$(1 + 1) \times (1 + 1) = 4$

In each case, several possibilities exist.

In the table below, how, using each number in the first column exactly four times, and by inserting between them just three of the arithmetical signs + - × ÷, can you obtain each of the numbers in the second column?

×	Numbers
2	0, 1, 2, 3, 4, 5, 6, 10, 12
3	3, 4, 5, 6, 7, 8, 9, 10
4	3, 6, 7, 8, 24, 28, 32, 48
5	3, 5, 6, 26, 30, 50, 55, 120

Solution on page 142

WOLF, A GOAT AND A CABBAGE

Accompanied by a wolf, a goat, and a cabbage, you must cross a river in order to get home. Unfortunately, you have a tiny boat which only permits you to transport a single load at a time. Therefore, during each trip, you must leave two unguarded on the riverbank while making the crossing. How will you manage to get all of them safely across, without one of them being eaten (the wolf will eat the goat, and the goat will eat the cabbage)?

Solution on page 143

PANCAKES

The baker must bake three wheat pancakes, but can only place two at a time in his oven.

Knowing that it requires 3 minutes of baking per side, what is the minimum time needed to bake the three pancakes?

Solution on page 144

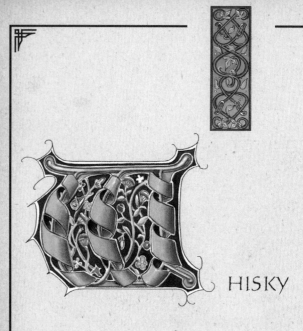 HISKY

What is unusual about this sentence?

'Did you know that Irish whiskey, often judged superior to the Scottish variety, existed from the beginning of the Middle Ages and quite often won prizes at medieval fairs?'

RABBIT FEET

Landry raises chickens and rabbits.
  When he counts heads, he finds eight.
  When he counts feet, he finds twenty-eight.
  How many rabbits does he have? And how many chickens?

Solution on page 146

 EAFNESS

The abbey's paschal candle has gone out and Friar
Benedict is charged with re-lighting it as soon as
he receives a signal from one of the three monks
located in the crypt beneath the abbey's chapel.

But Friar Benedict is a bit deaf from ringing the
abbey's bells, and only one of the three monks is
capable of yelling loud enough for Benedict to hear
him.

The abbot, who is also in the crypt, wants to
know which monk can do this. What must he do to
find out which monk Friar Benedict can hear, if he
only goes upstairs to the chapel once?

Note: the abbot cannot be helped by anyone else
and he cannot see into the chapel from the crypt.

Hints:
It is possible to check something else about the
candle other than whether or not it is alight. The
monks can ask Benedict to light it or to extinguish
it.

Solution on page 147

HE WORM IN THE MANUSCRIPT

A ten-volume manuscript is stored in the correct order on a library shelf.

Each volume is 4½ inches thick, with two covers, each ½ inch thick. A worm, starting on page 1 of volume I, eats its way in a straight line through the complete set and finishes on the last page of the last volume.

What distance does it travel in the course of its journey?

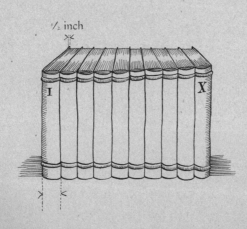

½ inch

Solution on page 148

ATCHES 2

This time, the alchemist's apprentice wants to move four matches to obtain three equilateral trangles that touch one another. No open or incomplete triangles must remain.

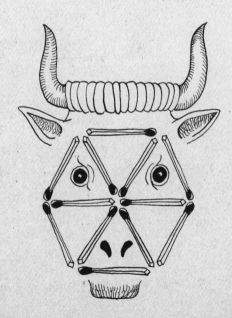

AT THE INN

A rag trader, a draper and a tapestry-maker, all on their way to the Stourbridge fair, stop off at an inn in Cambridge where they rent a room for three persons costing 30 pennies for the night.

Each of them thus gives 10 pennies. Since the innkeeper takes a liking to them, he reduces the price to 25 pennies and returns 5 pennies. But as there are three of them, they decide to take 1 penny each and to leave 2 pennies as a tip.

Each of them has paid 9 pennies $(3 \times 9 = 27)$ and the innkeeper has recovered 2 pennies.

$$27 + 2 = 29$$

Where did the thirtieth penny go?

Solution on page 150

EETING

Some monks leave Cluny abbey headed for the abbey at Clairvaux. An hour later, another group of monks leaves Clairvaux in the direction of Cluny.

Knowing that the first group walks 5 miles in an hour, while the second group advances at the slower pace of 3 miles per hour, which group of monks is closer to Cluny abbey when the two parties meet?

Solution on page 151

PREDICTION

Nostradamus announced the following:

'On Wednesday 2 February 2000, a world event will take place for the first time in over a thousand years, not seen since 28 August 888.'

What could he have meant?

Solution on page 152

 ARD BRAIN-TEASER

A tumbler draws three cards at random from a deck of fifty-two and lays them out before him.

Can you determine which cards these are, and their order, with the help of the following four clues?

Clue 1:
A 5 is to the right of a king
(but not necessarily next to it).

Clue 2:
A club is to the left of a spade
(but not necessarily next to it).

Clue 3:
A 10 is to the left of a heart
(but not necessarily next to it).

Clue 4:
A heart is to the left of a spade
(but not necessarily next to it).

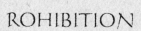ROHIBITION

Read this sign once and then turn quickly to the solution.

!

Please
leave your
weapons at
at the castle gates

Solution on page 154

 ORK

Here is a fork formed by four matches and containing marbles:

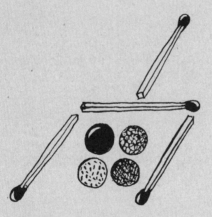

By shifting two matches, the fork has exactly the same shape, but the marbles are now outside it. Which matches should be moved to achieve this?

 IGITAL DISPLAY

On a clock with a digital display, how many times per day does the number 1 appear?

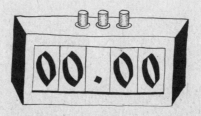

1 = 2 ?

Let's say a = 1, b = 1

a = b [1] Obviously!

a × a = a × b [2]

Multiply both sides of the equation by a.

a × a - b × b = a × b - b × b [3]

Subtract b x b from both sides.

a × a + a × b - a × b - b × b = b × (a - b) [4]

Add 0 = a × b - a × b on the left; we factorize b on the right.

a × (a + b) - b × (a + b) = b (a - b) [5]

Factorize twice (a and b) on the left.

(a + b) × (a - b) = b × (a - b) [6]

Factorize (a + b) on the left.

a + b = b [7]

Simplify.

2 = 1 [8]

And cry foul... Yes, but where is the error?

Solution on page 157

MPTY GLASS

How many drops of water can be put into an empty goblet?

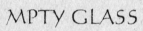

Solution on page 158

 UM OF 1 TO 100

Calculate the sum of the first one hundred whole numbers:

$1 + 2 + 3 + ... + 99 + 100 = ?$

Solution on page 159

ADDITION

How can you obtain 1,000 from a numerical addition containing only 8s?

Solution on page 160

INSHIP BOND

The father of my son = me (logical, isn't it?).
So the sentence becomes: 'If the son of this man, is "me",
what is the kinship bond between this man and me?'

Which is quite simple: this man is your father.

MILLION HAIRS

The answer is yes. If the number of inhabitants is greater than the maximum number of hairs on anyone's head, then there must be an insufficient number of 'hairs on head' for all of them to have a different number. Certain inhabitants of the kingdom of France must necessarily have the same numbers of hairs on their head.

And what about fleas?

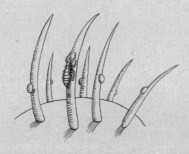

ANUSCRIPT

The pages of the manuscript bearing the number 9 are:
9-19-29-39-49-59-69-79-89-99 (be careful: there are two 9s in 99),
but also:
  90-91-92-93-94-95-96-97-98 which are often forgotten!
The cleric thus inscribes the number 9 20 times while
numbering the pages of the manuscript.

# ABRIC CLIPPING

Never! The diagonal lines are parallel, and therefore they can never meet. Do you find that disorientating?

Solution for page 13

SOLATION

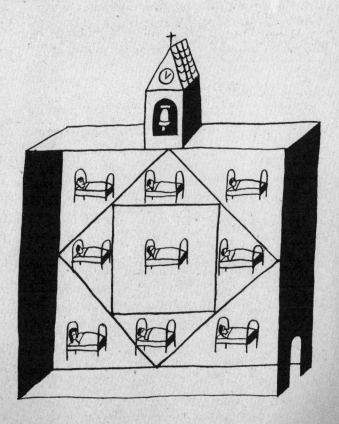

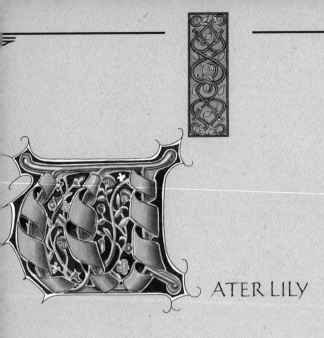

ATER LILY

It would take nine years.

Since each water lily doubles in surface area each year, the water lily that will completely cover the pond in the tenth year therefore covers half of it in the ninth year. The second water lily also covers half, so together they cover it completely.

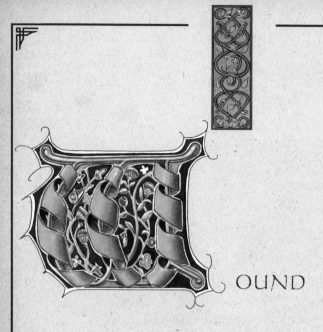

OUND

The doctor is his mother!

 ATS

The same three cats!
  If the three cats catch on average one mouse per minute, in one hundred minutes, they will catch one hundred mice.

Solution for page 17

TOURNAMENT

Only one person is heading for the tournament:

You!

Solution for page 18

ATCH TRIANGLES 1

All the carpenter's apprentice needs to do is to construct a Star of David (who said the triangles had to be all the same size?)

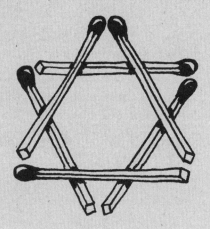

We often look for difficult answers to easy questions.

Solution for page 19

ATCH TRIANGLES 2

You need to think in 3D!

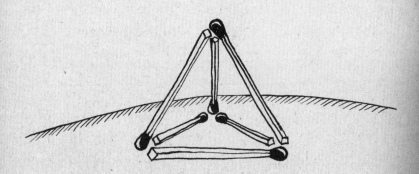

ICIOUS CIRCLE

Three won't do, because it contains an R.
  So the answer is four.
  The correct sentence is:
  'In this circle the "r." is present four times.'

HE MONK AND THE MOUNTAIN

The answer is yes. To make it obvious, suppose we have two monks who both depart at 9am: one starts from the bottom of the mountain and the other from the top. Since they are both on the same path, they will have to meet each other!

 TRANGE
EQUIVALENCE

In any period: 31 in octal (that is, in base 8) is always equal to 25 in the decimal system (that is, in base 10).

Base 10	Base 8	Base 10	Base 8
1 → 1		14 → 16	
2 → 2		15 → 17	
3 → 3		16 → 20	
4 → 4		17 → 21	
5 → 5		18 → 22	
6 → 6		19 → 23	
7 → 7		20 → 24	
8 → 10		21 → 25	
9 → 11		22 → 26	
10 → 12		23 → 27	
11 → 13		24 → 30	
12 → 14		25 → 31	
13 → 15		...	

Solution for page 23

 OVE POTION

At the end of step 6, there remains 4 fl oz in the 5 fl oz jar.

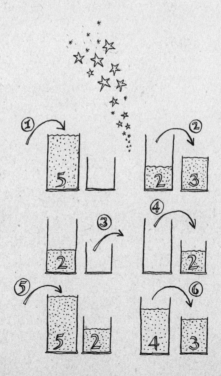

QUESTION OF AGE

State of affairs:

Age	Before	Now
Master	x	40
Pupil	y	z

What do we know?

• $40 = 4 \times y$ because 'I am four times as old as you were'
so $y = 10$

Age	Before	Now
Master	x	40
Pupil	10	z

• $z = x$ because 'I was the same age as you are now'

Age	Before	Now
Master	x	40
Pupil	10	z (or x)

• The difference in their ages is the same at any given time, so:

$x - 40 = 10 - x$

$2 \times x = 50$

$x = 25$ The pupil is therefore 25 years old.

Solution for page 25

SHIELD OF NAILS

UT-UP SQUARE

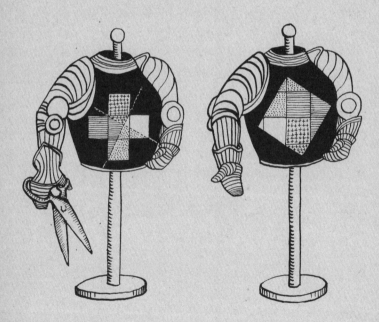

a black feather on my helmet

SINGLE FILE

Percival is the winner, affirming that there is a black feather on his helmet. His reasoning is as follows:

'I know that there are two black feathers and two white ones. Gawain can see me, so if my feather is the same colour as Galahad's, which he can also see, he would have deduced the colour of his own feather, which necessarily would have been different from ours. Since he remained silent, that means my feather is a different colour from Galahad's. I see that Galahad is wearing a white feather, so mine is black.'

UT-UP

 ELLS

The three seconds that go by in ringing four o'clock correspond to the intervals between bell tolls, not the number of tolls. To ring the twelve tolls of midday, Quasimodo will take eleven seconds, corresponding to the eleven intervals separating the twelve tolls of the bell.

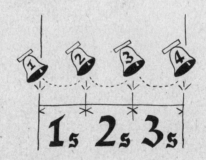

 IVE SQUARES

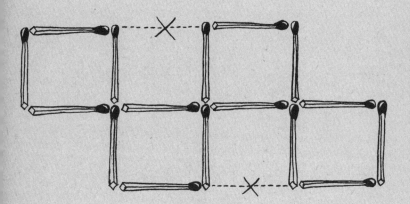

HILDREN

The other half of his children are also daughters!

 LOCK

When Aucassin leaves home, he winds up his clock and sets it to 12 o'clock. When he goes to see Nicolette, he looks at the clock on the façade of the church to note his time of arrival and his time of departure. When he returns home, he looks at his verge-and-foliot clock and then knows how much time he has spent away from home.

By subtracting the time he spent with his girlfriend, he knows how much time he spent walking…

By adding half of this time to the time he left Nicolette, he is able to tell what time it really is.

Solution for page 34

ALUE OF THE PRODUCT

The series is equal to 0 because $(x - x)$ equals 0.

Solution for page 35

 IVE ALIGNMENTS

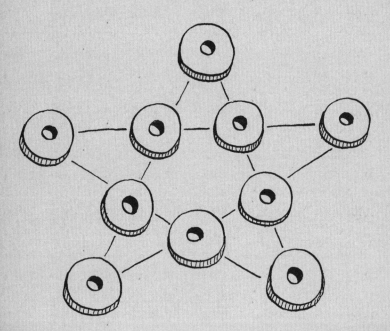

ROSE WINDOW

Neither, the two circles have the same diameter. Unusual, isn't it?

Case n° 1

Case n° 5

Case n° 2

Case n° 6

Case n° 3

Case n° 7

Case n° 4

EADDRESS

The lady reasons as follows:

Case no. 1: impossible because the first lady would have answered 'YES' upon seeing two white headdresses, since her own could only be black.

Case no. 2: impossible because the second lady would have answered 'YES' upon seeing two white headdresses, since her own could only be black.

Case no.3: impossible because the second lady would have answered 'YES', taking into account the response of the first lady (case no. 1), since her own headdress could only be black.

Case no. 4: possible case.

Case no. 5: possible case.

Case no. 6: possible case.

Case no. 7: possible case.

Conclusion: in the last four possible cases, the blind lady's headdress can only be black, allowing her to answer 'YES.'

HE GUARDS' HALL

In the Guards' Hall, there are as many weapons as
there are men, that is, 600.

   5% (or 30 of these men) carry one weapon. Among the
570 who remain, representing 95%, half of them carry
two and the other half carry none: that is the same
number of weapons as if they all carried one.

   Which gives 570 + 30 = 600 weapons.

ROUBADOUR

He juggles!

If he was juggling with the objects all the way across the bridge, there was always an object that was not actually in the troubadour's hands.

ISH

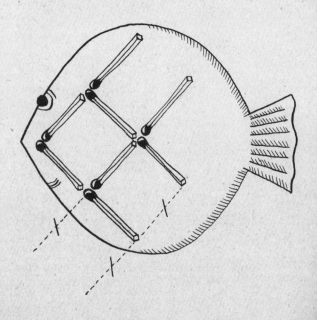

Solution for page 43

RIANGLE TRICK

Here's one solution:

CCURRENCES

To be true, the sentence must be completed in the following fashion:

'In this sentence, the number of occurrences of 0 is 1, of 1 is 7, of 2 is 3, of 3 is 2, of 4 is 1, of 5 is 1, of 6 is 1, of 7 is 2, of 8 is 1, and 9 is 1.'

The code for the strongbox is therefore: 1732111211
To start with the only certainty is that the number of 0s is 1. You must then solve this brain-teaser by trial-and-error, the quickest route being to examine the 9 next, then the 8...

THREE-WAY GAME

Since 9 is an odd number, Eberulf must have lost the last round. Before that round, their holdings were:
4 / 18 / 5 (round no. 5)

Same method for the preceding rounds:

Leander lost round no. 4, when each of them started with: 2 shillings (Martin), 9 shillings (Eberulf), and 16 shillings (Leander).

Eberulf lost round no. 3, when each of them started with: 1 shilling (Martin), 18 shillings (Eberulf), and 8 shillings (Leander).

Martin lost round no. 2, when each of them started with: 14 shillings (Martin), 9 shillings (Eberulf), and 4 shillings (Leander)

Eberulf lost round no. 1, when each of them started with: 7 shillings (Martin), 18 shillings (Eberulf), and 2 shillings (Leander).

A PLACE OF THEIR OWN

All you need to do is place them back to back!

HREE SWISS

The three Swiss are... women!

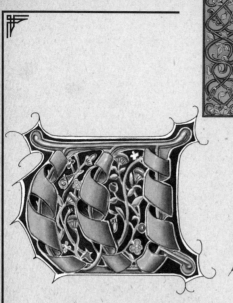

ATER IN THE WINE

Suppose that there was 80% water and 20% wine in the first mug at the end of the manoeuvre. The 20% of water that is missing must be in the other mug, as is the 80% of missing wine. To start with, there was the same amount of each liquid. The proportions in the second mug must thus be 20% water and 80% wine. The proportions are perfectly inverted: 80/20 as opposed to 20/80.

So there is as much wine in the first mug as there is water in the second, and as much wine in the second as there is water in the first.

HAT DAY?

Sunday

ATCHES 2

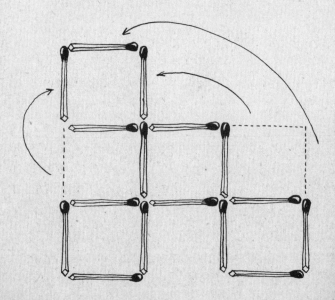

Solution for page 53

 USES

First of all, Merlin lights A, B, and C, at the same time.

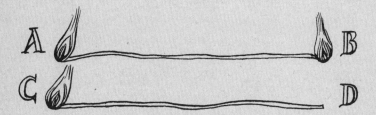

When the first fuse (A B) is entirely consumed, 30 minutes will have gone by. Merlin will then light D...

... and the 30 minutes of fuse (C D) remaining will be consumed in 15 minutes.
30 min + 15 min = 45 min.

Solution for page 54

TANDARD

The numbers 1 and 8 have a characteristic distinct from the rest: they are the only numbers to have just one neighbour (respectively 2 and 7).

  Following on from this, these two numbers are placed in the spaces at the centre of the standard (the ones with the greatest number of neighbours); then 2 and 7 are placed in the only spaces they can go in: these are the outermost spaces, 2 next to 8 and 7 next to 1. Lastly, the four remaining numbers are judiciously placed in the upper and lower spaces of the standard. One possible solution would be this:

And there you have it!

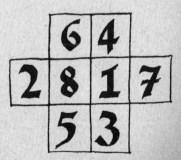

AVED COURTYARD

All the lines are perfectly straight.
Puzzling, isn't it?

Solution for page 56

BEAR HUNT

The bear is white. In fact, this phenomenon is only possible at the following places:

1. Exactly at the North Pole.

The 5 miles to the east are not straight in line: the route forms the arc of a circle while remaining at a distance of 5 miles from the pole (at each instant, one is moving eastwards). The bear is a polar bear, so it is white.

2. Let us imagine a latitude where it is possible to go around the world in 5 miles. These exist very near the South Pole and the North Pole. Near the North Pole, the hunter would be less than 5 miles from the pole, so it would not be possible to arrive there after travelling 10 km to the south. So let's look at the vicinity of the South Pole.

Consider a circle, parallel to the equator (that is to say, a circle of latitude), with a circumference of 5 miles, which goes around the world at this very location.

We depart from a point located 5 miles to the north of this circle. We travel 5 miles south (so we find ourselves on this circle), 5 miles east (we go around the world and find ourselves back at the preceding position), then 5 miles north (we find ourselves back at the starting point).

The second solution is therefore: all the points located on a circle 5 miles to the north of a second circle 5 miles in circumference, in the Southern hemisphere. But as we all know, there aren't any bears, polar or otherwise, living in the Antarctic...

ARSENIC

All the queen needs to do is to number the twelve boxes 1 to 12, from left to right. Then she must take:
- 1 pill from box 1
- 2 pills from box 2
- 3 pills from box 3

etc.
- 12 pills from box 12

Finally, she weighs all of the pills removed from the boxes, or 78 pills in all. If all of them were purely medicinal, they would weigh:

$78 \times 10 = 780$ oz

Knowing that a pill of arsenic weighs 1 oz less, all she has to do is calculate the difference between 780 oz and the result. For example, if the queen finds 777 oz, it's box 3 (from which she took 3 pills) that contains the arsenic.

It looks like the king's favourite's days are... numbered!

ISHING

In fact there are three people who go fishing, not four: grandfather, father and the latter's son - who constitute two fathers accompanied by their sons.

Solution for page 59

ONNECTIONS

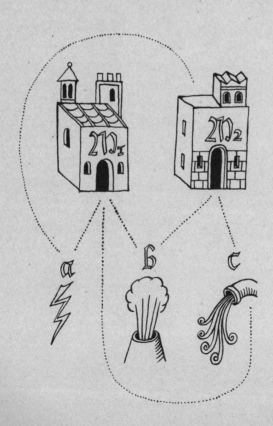

ROMAN NUMERAL EQUATION 1

It has to be read backwards:

Solution for page 62

ROMAN NUMERAL EQUATION 2

(The square root of 1 equals 1.)

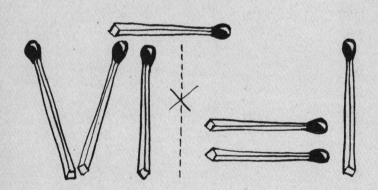

Solution for page 63

RIANGLE AND SUMS

On the 1-2 side, we are missing 14 which we can get from either 5 + 9 or 6 + 8.

On the 2-3 side, we are missing 12 which we can get from either 4 + 8 or 5 + 7.

On the 1-3 side, we are missing 13 which we can get from either 4 + 9, or 5 + 8, or 6 + 7.

By elimination, that gives:

side 1-2: 5 + 9
side 2-3: 4 + 8
side 1-3: 6 + 7

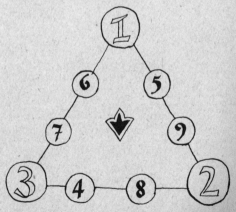

Solution for page 64

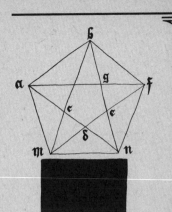

OUNT THE TRIANGLES

There are two types of straight line here: those of the pentagon and those of the star. Let's start by considering those triangles having a side in common with the pentagon. For a given side NM, we can make six triangles (points A, B, C, D, E, and F).

If we apply this observation to the five sides in rotation, we see that certain triangles are counted twice: those which have two sides in common with the pentagon. If we exclude the triangle formed with point F (triangle NMF), there are no triangles counted twice. There are thus five triangles per side of the pentagon: twenty-five triangles are accounted for this way.

We have now dealt with all the cases of triangles having one side in common with the pentagon. The other triangles only have sides on the star. Consider the segment AN. Apart from triangles having sides in common with the pentagon, we can identify the triangles CDM and ANG. These are the only triangles possible without one side in common with the pentagon. Triangles of these two types are repeated five times in rotation around the figure. So we have ten more triangles here.

In all therefore, we have thirty-five triangles.

Solution for page 65

LAZIERS

Here is one possible solution:

ASSWORD

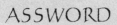

The papal legate should reply, 'Five,' which corresponds to the number of letters in the number pronounced by the guard.

 OME MENTAL
CALCULATIONS

$2 + 2 - 2 - 2 = 0$

$(2 \div 2) \times (2 \div 2) = 1$

$(2 \div 2) + (2 \div 2) = 2$

$(2 + 2 + 2) \div 2 = 3$

$2 + 2 + 2 - 2 = 4$

$2 + 2 + (2 \div 2) = 5$

$(2 \times 2 \times 2) - 2 = 6$

$(2 \times 2 \times 2) + 2 = 10$

$(2 + 2 + 2) \times 2 = 12$

$(3 + 3 + 3) \div 3 = 3$

$((3 \times 3) + 3) \div 3 = 4$

$3 + 3 - (3 \div 3) = 5$

$3 + 3 + 3 - 3 = 6$

$3 + 3 + (3 \div 3) = 7$

$(3 \times 3) - (3 \div 3) = 8$

$(3 \times 3) + 3 - 3 = 9$

$(3 \times 3) + (3 \div 3) = 10$

$((4 \times 4) - 4) \div 4 = 3$

$((4 + 4) \div 4) + 4 = 6$

$4 + 4 - (4 \div 4) = 7$

$(4 \times 4) - 4 - 4 = 8$

$(4 \times 4) + 4 + 4 = 24$

$(4 \times 4) \times 4 - 4 = 28$

$(4 \times 4) + (4 \times 4) = 32$

$(4 + 4 + 4) \times 4 = 48$

$(5 + 5 + 5) \div 5 = 3$

$((5 - 5) \times 5) + 5 = 5$

$((5 \times 5) + 5) \div 5 = 6$

$(5 \times 5) + (5 \div 5) = 26$

$(5 + (5 : 5)) \times 5 = 30$

$(5 \times 5) + (5 \times 5) = 50$

$((5 + 5) \times 5) + 5 = 55$

$(5 \times 5 \times 5) - 5 = 120$

Solution for page 69

A WOLF, A GOAT AND A CABBAGE

You must first cross with the goat and leave it on its own while you cross back.

Then you must bring over the wolf and come back with the goat.

You leave the goat and cross over with the cabbage.

Lastly, you return alone to the bank you started from and transfer the goat.

PANCAKES

The baker must bake three pancakes, each with two sides, which we will call a and b.

The quickest way to bake the three pancakes is as follows.

step 1: pancake 1 side a, and pancake 2 side a

step 2: pancake 2 side b, and pancake 3 side a

step 3: pancake 1 side b, and pancake 3 side b

With each step lasting 3 minutes, it will take 9 minutes for the baker to bake the three pancakes.

Note: other solutions exist, all involving the same number of steps.

Solution for page 71

 HISKY

This sentence uses all twenty-six letters of the alphabet.

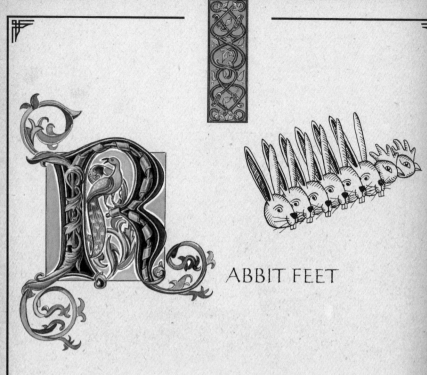

ABBIT FEET

Let x be the number of chickens and y the number of rabbits.

The number of heads is therefore $x + y$ and equals 8.

The number of feet is therefore $2x + 4y$ and equals 28.

Therefore:

[1] $x + y = 8$

[2] $2x + 4y = 28$

Equation [1] gives us: $x = 8 - y$ [3]

If we use this to replace x in [2], we get:

$2 (8 - y) + 4y = 28$

$16 - 2y + 4y = 28$

$2y = 12$

$y = 6$

From equation [3], we get:

$x = 2$

Landry has two chickens and six rabbits.

Solution for page 73

DEAFNESS

The abbot should proceed as follows:
- he must tell the first monk to give the signal to light the candle, wait 2 minutes then ask him to give another signal to extinguish the candle;
- he must then tell the second monk to give the signal to light the candle, and go up himself to check on things in the chapel:
  - if the candle is lit, Friar Benedict heard the second monk,
  - if the candle is out, but the abbot can see a little melted wax, Friar Benedict heard the first monk,
  - if the candle is out and cold, this means that Friar Benedict can only hear the third monk.

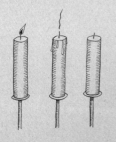

HE WORM IN THE MANUSCRIPT

The worm will have travelled 40½ inches, not 49½ inches.

The first page of volume 1 and the last page of volume X are not at the extremities of the set of books.

If you have trouble seeing this, take a book after having determined the location of the first page and place it upright on your bookshelf. You may be surprised!

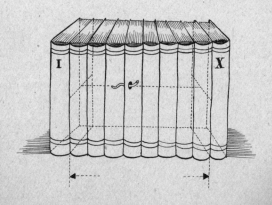

ATCHES 3

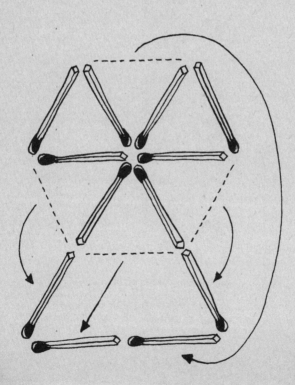

 T THE INN

The problem lies in the final sum: 27 + 2 = 29
At the end of the exchanges, the distribution is the following:

- Innkeeper: 27 pence, of which:
  Price of the room: 25 pence
  Tip: 2 pence
- Rag trader: 1 penny
- Draper: 1 penny
- Tapestry-maker: 1 penny

Nothing is lost.

The two pennies in the sum 27 + 2 = 29 are already part of the 27.

27 (of which 2 [tip] and 25 [room]) + 3 [clients] = 30 [total]

or again:

30 [total] - 3 [clients] - 2 [tip] = 25 [room]

All is well!

EETING

Since they meet, the two groups of monks will obviously both be at the same distance from Cluny at the moment of their meeting!

PREDICTION

02/02/2000 marks the first time since 28/08/888 when all the numbers of the date were even.

ARD BRAIN-TEASER

Thanks to clues 1 and 3, we know that the cards we seek are a king, a 5, and a 10.

It only remains to determine their suit and their place. From clue 2, we can propose three hypotheses:

 This hypothesis is eliminated by clue 4.

 This hypothesis is eliminated by clue 3.

 This hypothesis is therefore the correct one.

Lastly, we know from clue 3 that the 10 is to the left of the heart, and from clue 1 that the 5 is to the right of the king. The answer is therefore:

Solution for page 80

PROHIBITION

Strangely, most people don't see the repetition of the word 'AT.'

Solution for page 82

 ORK

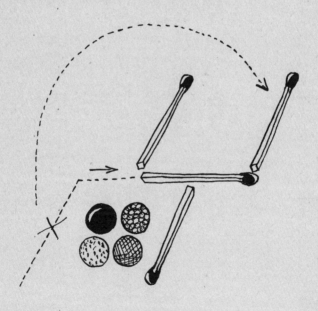

IGITAL DISPLAY

In the course of a day, the display goes from 0:00 to 23:59.

Twelve hours of the day contain the number 1:

1:00	13:00	17:00
10:00	14:00	18:00
11:00	15:00	19:00
12:00	16:00	21:00

Moreover, in the course of the same hour, the number 1 appears fifteen times at the following minutes:

hr:01	hr:16	hr:51
hr:10	hr:17	
hr:11	hr:18	
hr:12	hr:19	
hr:13	hr:21	
hr:14	hr:31	
hr:15	hr:41	

Therefore, for a 24-hour day this gives us:

24 × 15 = 360 occurrences

360 + 12 = 372

In all, the number 1 thus appears 372 times in the course of a day.

Solution for page 84

$$1 = 2 ?$$

The error is located between line 6 and line 7.

We divided by (a - b)... which is equal to 0. Division by 0 is, of course, impossible.

MPTY GLASS

Only one, because after that, the goblet is no longer empty!

Solution for page 86

 UM OF 1 TO 100

We know that:
1 + 100 = 101
2 + 99 = 101
etc.

So the sum equals:
50 × 101 = 5,050
Seen in another way:
$1 + 2 + 3 + ... + (n - 1) + n = n(n + 1) \div 2$
with n = 100
$1 + 2 + 3 + ... + 100 = 100 \times 101 \div 2 = 5,050$

Solution for page 87

DDITION

$$8 + 8 + 8 + 88 + 888 = 1000$$

Solution for page 88